This Black-ideology

This Black-ideology

Anthology of Poems by a Black Child

Sternly K` Simon

authorHOUSE®

AuthorHouse™
1663 Liberty Drive
Bloomington, IN 47403
www.authorhouse.com
Phone: 1-800-839-8640

First published by AuthorHouse   06/27/2011

ISBN: 978-1-4567-8214-6 (sc)
ISBN: 978-1-4567-8213-9 (ebk)

Printed in the United States of America

Contents

Cultivating Palatable Soils

Phenomena

Until . . . the End

A Secrets Told To 1 is All

His Fables

This Black-ideology

This Black-ideology

This book is dedicated to all poetry enthusiasts, poeters and poetess, readers and digesters of literature work in its kind.

Acknowledged will be the likes of Goitseone Dollen Montshiwa, Tshepiso Nancy Simon, Sithembile Dube, Asalepele Omphile, Olebile Serge Mogobe, Abu Al Yessr Mohamed El Amin Suliman, Zalina Binti Ismail, Viera Linderova and Anita Kulon for all your contribution. I appreciate the inspiration, encouragement you gave me and your long anticipation for me to publish my work. Motivation of this book, is from my late mother and brother Mavis Mareledi Montshiwa and Christopher Khumoetsile Montshiwa respectively for their memory lives on with me.

Also many thanks to the father I have never known to exist in my life because I wonder if he is dead or alive. Just being thoughtful thanks for bringing me into this world.

To all my friends, acquaintances, colleagues and family thanks for the support.

Love you all.

Incognito of my poetry

Incognito of my poetry
Concise to your point
Rapture my brain to tumour
Captured audience made sale
Published without vague critics
Sharp edged forwarded none masquerade
Notable in key by Debussy Claude
Masochistic to Ovid and Vatsayana
Metamorphoses

Wind chimes embrace atmosphere of my poetry
Famous the words yet the poet is
Young and vibrant
Black and immaculate
With a stance and charms
Switched on to incognito mode of the poem

Incognito of my poetry
Notorious pounder of English-tongue
Correlation between bow-down and salute
Orally reverberated to you
Generated dictionary term to merge my thoughts in pen
Noted in the manner of utterance killing the muted voice of a
black child
Illustrating style and passion of poetry as a creative art
Teaching that shall be manifested in literature
Ordained to the readers of then, now and there

My Mystical Writing

Mysteries of my mystical writing in misery
quoting my deeply withheld thoughts and my dismay
something peculiar about me must be amiss

reminiscing about my renaissances of love
maybe my delinquency to love has me love-sick
because I casted mine eyes down,
dreading to gaze at this sick world

Brave hearted son of Africa enchanted by my charms and
incantations
this rich syllables my original recitation is obsession in its kind
oblivious of my wretched sins and . . . Devious mentality
in my pitfalls a poet is unleashed

I spoke a word or two and . . .
married ink and paper in holy matrimony
played with metaphors, similes and rhymes
my utterance, the linguistics of the spoken word

in the mist of my mystical writing
memories of my lost-love come back to haunt me
prudent in handling my matters of the heart
I know love suffice a man like a mother's womb
it brings me happiness and call my pursuit to a halt

I step down propaganda of me in my mystical writing
making you listen and read as I speak of my mind in misery

I spoke a word or two and . . .
Married ink and paper in holy matrimony
played with metaphors, similes and rhymes
my utterance, the linguistics of the spoken word

This is for the Others

others may look but can never embrace this
others took it for granted because of this
others have a book same but different from this
others matter than you do and why is this
others painted their hurt hearts anxiety in this
others told the new corners of this world about this

others lost fortunes invested just for this
others gave almighty God a frown because they could not find
this
others dance at its feet with charms likes this
others go insane to loose this

others bother their mother's womb to get out of this
others the last time I checked despised and hated this
others chased the wind in vain to catch this
others cried waterfalls of Victoria falls over this

others with less knowledge or may be IQ, press charges against this
others portrayed patriotic mind set of this
others blamed mama Africa, for what was this is this!!

others set on a solid rock waiting on this
others like you and me stand perplexed of this
others read but not all depicted what this poem meant by this
others re-sighted the misinterpretation of this
others knew this is for the others
because we are not all like this
We are better than this
Don't you reckon this?

Reality

These baffled thoughts seem blur to this vivid reality
rigid they stand rooted in their awkward divinity
whilst letting their troubles hold them down in captivity
who could have lucid theory, of that kind of mentality
Un-ruled un-governed destiny
Because they possess vanity

begging for pardon in their disloyalty
the real world suffered their brutality
in their levity
They claim to sovereignty
haughty
As they view this reality
Unworthy

this reality is that and that
it is now!
It is now, writing the next chapter of their tomorrow
In quantity equivalent to quality
Of letters for word are plenty
for today it has perused through

This Black-ideology

their page 1
of their bruised hearts maybe
that daily routine
contrary to the moments that passed
with yesterday
Such was a lovely day
that is bygone for reality has taken
charge on the future

in the real world
Missing fantasy and dreams
such is life
presentation of facts not fables is reality
Past is history
Of now reality

Lie In The Truth

The
Truth is that, truth lies to tell off lies
The truth would not hurt if it was on its own
It seems lies hurt like the truth that was told
Or when it was not said, a lie said something, at least
And that's where the name liar comes from
You see the truth witnessed all lies a liar could device
When the liar stand corrected by the truth
Just to make matters worse, of lies said before
The
Truth is, Lie and Truth are a syndicate
In conviction, "truth or dare"
Lie also known as blue lie, he is really
A true liar, conning in his own way
He got the truth to shamefully tell the truth
After he lied, only to be embarrassed
For the truth was already known, to be told
The
Truth is, to listen when the truth is telling us the whole truth
Guess the remain truth is possibly lies;
Funny huh, it seems we listen to both of them in either case
We'll still listen so attentively to lie telling us lies
The
Truth is that, truth will set us free
Perhaps reality would object to that, I object too
Lies can bail the truth out, without a cent spent
Jail is not their place to be, I tell you
We have a room for each of them in us
And our claim contradicts to hate a liar . . .

When he is our accomplice to lie more and more
Where the truth does not reside
Lies stand afraid that the truth will come out one day
And the
Truth is, we never forget the truth like we wake up
When we are not dead
But since lies don't have a good liar
They tend to forget the lie and lies of close relative lies
Because the clan of Lies is big, it's a family tree
Of cousin Lie, cousin Lie, cousin Lies,
Lie,
Lie,
Lie, Lie, and Lie
This lies even have grandparents named Lie, so I hear
And their last name is pronounced "Lie"
To end my poem here
Before I delude your mind with my theory
Lies are lies full stop

12 months

Be redeemed from all my lies and deceit; **January**

secrets shadowed by my charms you will forfeit; **February**

trust you embedded on my sketch painting on; **March**

while I fade away in your undying thoughts of me; **April**

let it go don't try to elicit a solution; **May**

where we will find no resolution; **June**

in the outskirts of our ruins; **July**

it shall only bring you a tear to drop; **August**

and how I hate to see you cry dear; **September**

clear enough I have no right to make you cry; **October**

pry your eyelids to the falling skies at 9t; **November**

on a full moon you'll see me,
coming around from there like a shooting star; **December**

just to love you like I never did for; **12 months**

Black Child

The things u do

the things u do don't amuse a few not even a million

you leave your life at their expectations like you are on the edge
of the world

what do you expect when street lights shine away from you

your shadow not resembling who you are

your foot print dnt leave a mark

do you know who you are

the things you do don't respect nature

then you say mother earth has turned her back on you

when the path you choose leads no way

you will always get a ticket if you keep the fast lane

change the ways you think

poetry that I write you c yourself like the mirror

3 little birds sing songs of sorrow

a dedication when you raise and don't shine in the eyes of your
Lord

you run when no one is chasing after you

stop and realize life does not end at the cross roads

its only the beginning not a dead end

the things you say scares me

the next thing you want to take your life by the string

you keep your evil ways n stay away from me

at the end of the tunnel you see no light that a blind can even see
with his sixth sense

find yourself soon before judgement day

may be dear lord will spare you a sit next to him in heaven

the things you do lead to hell

drink the water before the well runs dry

when your poor mother cries a bucket full as u waste your future

Sternly K` Simon

realize the confusion you living in
do you want to diffuse or flow with the wind that ends at—ve
infinity
no one can help u if u don't help yourself
now you know things u do shocks more than earthquake

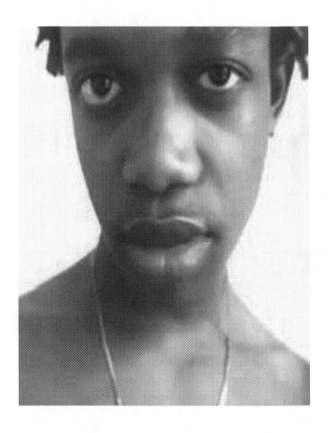

Living true Ignorantly

i need a size king boot and a khaki suite
to stand up for the truth and represent the youth
give me a strong reggae beat tune
to chant down babylon for their evil doing
Lord amplify my voice against racism and fascism
give praise and condemn; negative virtue, respective to be known
as vice
let no bad deed go unpunished oh Lord
this is the people's court!

Judge Together we stand divided we Fall preceding
I see no difference between both of you freedom fighters
you both following the same thing,
that has been and still is
keeping down black people.

I need ink on scroll paper
to write this message to my Lord in bold

Lord I see fusing and fighting
bullets missing targets of our own brothers, killing the innocent
ones
apartheid in disguise, whites shredding blacks into pieces
criticism and racism prevailing in the 1st world
blacks fear is growing deep in the roots of the 3rd world
afraid is the black child to set foot out of Africa
should we regret the brains that flew us to Asia, Europe, America
when justice is not served; where is my ambassador
this world is false to us blacks when we are living true ignorantly

Sternly K`Simon

loud as roaring lions I hear their prayers in my deep sleep
in different tongues not of my mother tongue
mute as if I have no voice cords I can't pray as they
some call us minorities who gave them the right
freedom comes to those who fight not those who cry
and party hoping they will dance their problems away
free yourselves black man in this revolution when you read the
Revelation
Lord made us all equal; non is superior neither inferior to one kind
let no man treat you like trash because only HIM has the power
nonsense I rebuke sternly
hostility I burn down with words of wisdom

to be continued . . . .

Um only African

From birth I was persecuted
In my childhood I was sold
In my youth was enslaved
For I am only African
Born in the battle ground
Born in the sea of starvation and famine
Born in the core of racial discrimination
For I am AFRICAN
In the world of thick darkness
I grew up
in the world of unbearable agony
I was bred
For I am AFRICAN
In the world of chaotic chaos
I fought with courage
Brothers are late
Afro centrism preserved my life

Vile

when you boast it goes with your incomparable frown in the
mirror
the arrogance elevated from what used to be known to be a
person in you
deludes in-comprehensively the nature of the man you where
bond to become
for your scornful smile is holding anger detained captive in you
in the name of Satan Lucifer son of the devil,
I swear,
when your hate is unleashed, it will be like hell fires
burning down serenity synonyms being tranquillity will be ashes
to dust
because this people can't stand the manifestation of your
rudeness
it has abominated their shallow faith in God; what a vile humour
when you use vile language before the ears of their growing
children
such is another vile slander for a grownup like you to be
tolerated

how can you surrender a lie before the truth could be told
of your vile deeds and protruding mischievous behaviour
in the same act, devious to all good
and the people you shall call your parents are perpetrators
following vandalism of your own future, deemed crazy in
recognition
or perhaps mad insane,
vicious circle of sarcasm begins with you
cursing your mother and father, misfortune of an orphan

don't hate the world
it will see you until the bitter end
of your idea to tormenting and hurting the innocent Godly
children of Israel
description of your kind comes close to the heartless syndicate
of the merciless
and you don't care.
Shame following you like a shadow
righteousness building upon your wickedness like Tag Mahal
who said you are like a leaning Tower of Pisa in Rome
when you fall you will be miserable,
embarrassed for trying to conquer love with hate

Take a gaze around, none but a few pronounce you with envy
because many more like you have faded away like melanin of an
albino
you don't intend to change my friend as though sins cannot be
confessed
before his almighty, to be granted forgiveness is better than to
be condemned
respect of a man comes with no pity, its earned
be a good person, is not that difficult like a nut that wont crack
open.

The Journey Continues

the journey seems far beyond the end of your perspective
respectively is your mind setting you backward
your thought running wild helter-skelter
and your wits failing you like life support machine
when you can't carry on nor more who is letting you down
then you frown to the babies who know less of the troubles of your
heart desires
let them lead their own destiny and you flow suite

you ran your race and is still on
you had your dreams and you did not leave them
you nature mammal God brought to this earth, blood clotted
your veins
you left opportunities of life times death miss you not by chance
you gave chase to the winds of your cyclone hopes to the west
and your anticyclone wishes to the east
what did you write back home about you hopeless human times
infinity in vanity
all your effortless strive in this journey, a disgrace to humanity
fade away you condemned mankind by the trinity
Pray for you have forsaken your sanity
The great calamity has been your bad choices in life
Liberate your capability from captivity
You lack of decency icon of men earn your dignity
you ran your race and is still on
You had your dreams and you did not leave them
You nature mammal God brought to this earth, blood clotted
your veins
You left opportunities of life time's death miss you not by chance

This Black-ideology

You gave chase to the winds of your cyclone hopes to the west
And your anticyclone wishes to the east
Your water fall tears we pity you
As they flow down streams of Okavango river
prior to your shame came fame marching in your shadow
Shadow your negative attitude with positive-ness towards this prophesied journey
it was written . . . .
Every men shall walk and run, this journey
Dead souls have taken, this journey
Look down on your selflessness for your ancestors are not proud of you
when your journey continues . . . . in vain

Black Child

lets create this being that is dominately stereotyped
prejudiced to his cause of color missing in the rainbow nation
racially discreminated from the abondant history of slavery
impoverishment of his kind,not accepted by westerners
washed out into his land, in canoes like boats
perpetrators in shadows of spreading the gospel of the trinity
they were entitled to be deemed norm as missionaries
them manipulating the terms traitors with traders of barter
system
the idea seemed entriguingly too good to be true, for betterment
Until they took what rightously belonged to thee and him in slave
ships
his soul right treasures of the land ravished once upon a time till
today
it happened;,
as a black child we used to be excited to see a white person
pass through our villages,towns and shanty townships
we would run behind their unpaved shoeprints with our
barefootprints
in everblazing heat of our mother land soil, and thorns
just to touch their white skin was amazingly appeasing to us,
at the time we had not borrowed the enlish tongue
so we could not speak, but drew a broadway smile of excitment
across our oblivious faces, eyes glowing iris pure white with a
brown pupil
Utterly black is not a color destintive to bare a black child in this
segragation
surely its preposterous for humanity to condone this sarcasm in
this day and time

we could afford to raise our next generation where racism does not prevail

entertaining interracial relationships with annotations from this words

setting aside any peculiar thought of one being different in somewhat sort.

Yes! its happening;.

see a black child on board to abroad overseas and valleys

perceived as what is depicted in the media about Africa, where he comes from

then your malititude delibarately made sure he remains to taste the anguish

and suffering, whilst already overwhelmed by it and the shrugs you give to him

only bolds the pride, of how he got here in the 1st place.

he hold virtuous the cross that you have been brain washed to hate black people.

Nor shall you be blamed for your actions against any black child.

Inspite solitude setted

solidarity would welcome a black child in the march of your disciples

tables where you dine, serve him the meals for a change in glassware,

silver spoons, forks and knifes, including the delicacy of them

starters and deserts, chop sticks no can't do . . .

will continue from here next time travellers

if you comprehend what the poet is on to . . .

Without Sonnet

This poem

This poem has seen many reckless drivers of their own unjust life
Their forgone opportunities maybe their distress
They dress to kill but they are left out of their fortress
Then broadcast their mischief opinions like the press
This poem will not impress but depress

This poem is a significance of my existence
This words are filthy rich than sixpence
Mind not the tense used but the sentence made

Um not the false preacher who needs deliverance
yet stands in front of the congregation for the gospel
The denomination is misled with a bad spell
This rebel forfeit to the devil dynasty and this poem shall tell
Black Child is the teacher

This poem is a correction of contradiction
The clamours of our ancestors will be our rejection
The rumours of 3rd world war is conspiracy at its most
saturation
Their world policy of peace perpetrate justice delinquency
The calamity of change is this poem concentration
The power of death is eviction of man for his destruction

This poem is replacement of wrong management
Condemned will be the government of "Mugabe"
Oppressed will be those in power for rearrangement in the hierarchy
Pardoned will be many more like "Nelson Mandela" from imprisonment
Revealed will be corruption in the system brought to judgment
Saluted will be nonetheless man like Martin Luther King, with his good sentiment, and
Marcus Mosiah Garvey with the foundation of the Rastafari movement

This poem represents a way for the lost ones
Let them not go astray but do not worry about them for you will find no gain
Again and again telling them won't do it's a waste of words
Pain of consequences not felt is a waste of decision making
Rain of shared cries is a waste of tear drops
Insane is writing this poem a waste of my lines

This poem is moving on not looking back
This poem has pictured the future not history
This poem is deep rooted like our forefathers
This poem will be read till the end of times

For the lost ones

for the lost ones
This aches to the bones
Ear drum busted by stereo headphones
Balls between the legs deliver clones
Kings on the throne wearing crowns
The Pope listening to your confessions in many tones
Two wrongs don't make right in several tongues

for the lost ones
Italian red bull is upholding you to the rising moon between its hones
Claiming to be gangster like Al'capone
Fornicating around in different area codes leaving no unturned stones

for the lost ones . . . .
The burden on your shoulders weigh tonnes
Never can you last name be Bond to James
With your accomplice licking ice-cream cones
You miss called the Lord seventy times seven on public-phones

for the lost ones
With high level testosterone's and estrogens'
Is the chemistry of attraction of hormones
The lost ones
The drone's and Crone's
I've met many of you clowns
In crowds of fools like the lost ones

Sternly K` Simon

Her heart is Pure and Clean

Africa's conscious heart, never curse, nor befall a soul
Her heart is pure and clean
when they took what was rightfully hers by force
It was their rat race, and
At the end of the war and struggle we all rejoice
But they never seize fire . . . . racism and fascism . . .

it continues . . . .

Enemy lines in conjunction
Territory barriers at every junction
The story unfolds,
Babylon tricks won't function
Nation building is the way forward in determination
Their hidden agendas and ongoing system needs correction
love shared is the release of this tension and
She stands up and takes action, to claim her rightful place

Starting with, the wretched sin that Africa
. . . . stand un-haunted to confess before HIS eyes
Her heart is pure and clean
With prejudice they enslave
. . . . the blackness in our forefathers
and this hear my African brothers
is not ha . . . ha . . . ha . . . ha funny
all their evilous regimes . . . all against blacks

talk about apartheid the Ku Klux Klan
the depopulation of Africa chains of Slavery
the merciless killing and blooding shedding

They came, they took, her black man to fight their war
They colonized Africa when she was pregnant, and
They burned away her culture to ashes
Now her children speak in tongues for they lost their mother
tongue
Their books corroded her black child's mind with propaganda

It is a catastrophe in her land
but Her heart remains pure and clean
Her name is African, cannot be changed nor tamed
Her heart is pure and clean

Music elements

he said;

acoustic strumming strings break
are you the bass drum beat in my chest
the off drums snare
Crescendo in my heart
harmonics of piano sound is in your voice whisper
is it percussion

she replied;

strobelite of seduction is the calypso
the tonic is me

intertwined in broken chords
of your staccato tune of our rhythmic love
but you are melodious wind chimes down down down
my dear that tingling is crescendo

he said;

if i said i love you saxophone
would you say um a sextuple meter
tempo indicating vivaciousness in my eyes looking at you
melody of my voice could be modulated fermaaata
written in violin chords of a love note 2u
chorus melody of us legato

she said;

boy i hear your orchestra
musical elements of your love for me
overwhelming expression of feelings on a tambourine
you learned to get me dancing to your gong (tam-tam)
lyrics of your beautiful compliments in soprano
if you are proposing um saying YES with a French Horn
over my mezzo-soprano voice you will hear viola strings

he said;

my voice can be mellower than the dramatic baritone
my hands are softer than Albonini's Adagio
come let me be with you, like music of the baroque
we will compose our acapella in romanticism
musical elements, the likes of Antonin Dvorak and Franz Liszt

A Beautiful Poem

A beautiful poem was written
Uttered in a monophonic tone
Yet so lovely it tuned you to fall in sync with it
Turning you pink your favourite colour
Yes the beholder had
A voice so enchanting, so tantalizing, you know
It evokes that incredible smile you withhold
From the poet himself
Liberating words from his saliva lubricated brown lips
Which caress the mood
Which does come not to go
Like the false clouds that gathered
Giving you empty promises of nice showers of
Love rain drops but in vain
No this poem is really a true dedication to you
For you, are a pleasant look
For its beautiful like the curves cure of you black woman
Adorably more than a few embrace its pure
Captivated message sanctioned to bring back compliments
In abundance to flatter you
Appealing sense of remedial poem for the ugly also,
Their beauty lies within treasured to be found
Rested in a red velvet fitted sheet, with
A nice silk yellow touch of patterns, blending
With pink, purple blue roses
Dressing her inside beauty, i hear
With inviting scent of an African woman
You are.
You have,

White angel like butterflies around your shoulders
Walking in an immaculately manner
You queen of Eden
You are a daisy blossom in spring, shine in summer
White snow in winter and come autumn
This beautiful poem shall not scribble anything from here . . .
Because the poet dread to see your beauty fall like
Dry leaves to the season
of a brown carpet ground made of this leaves that seem
to resemble your caramel skin
which make you look so beautiful still like this poem

Cultivating Palatable Soils

Break up now or never

i am listening to my head and
you've been speaking wind chimes,
the melody that brought by my silence spree.
i figured you've been
seeing me a lot
talking to me a lot,
we should break up NOW

the knot we tied to imprison our mind
not to listen to our sub-consciousness
perhaps for you it was infatuation
that obsessed the nature of you
to hold on unto hope
faith there but only
blasphemous love

lacking synonyms famous as cliché's
i love you,
then cometh that part i ought to mumble back;
i love you too
Blink to the mere truth blind
i was only dearly lusting for you
posturised in display of mine eyez then
you killed it

Sternly K`Simon

the thing that we had was corals
divers and snorkeler's envied
it took me this long to read through your calligraphy
stolen from time, fine
you are slick like sand through the hour glass

metaphor yours calligraphy is
engraved with stencils of conniving graffiti character
behind the phenomenon of your disguised beautiness
the art of lying and deceit was named after you
nor the calamity that befalled me
when you walked gracefully into my heart
like the flight was nice but we hate the jet-lag
from a single celibate cloud

you clouded mine five star sensibility
to hear you attentively
to touch you inevitably
to smell you exultingly
to taste you diligently
to see you effeminately

we should break up NOW before we shag and make up
elongating stress
"we can give it another try"
i'll be damned over force to even consider the place
you ruined have a chance for repair,
not by you my dearest ice queen
i like islands called beaches paradise

Repatriation of love

excitation of this reverberation
is deep than essence of penis penetration
yawning suave soothing vibration of music
in your tense stance this is the revelation

if you were hostile to the declaration of love
now find the meaning from many translation
i shall not change the definition of love
not even in my might, frustration that will come
humongous reconciliation of self-mortification

Upon sanity you and i face crucifixion
feelings of ardent love; devotion
that never dies
that never hates nor curse
and if i love you; then i will let you go

skimming in the section of our page 1
when we 1st met, then rain clouds gathered
it was too good to last a generation
should it become infestation
i rather be feel the fires of cremation and pain

than to let your deception keep me holding on in vain
to "i love you"
to "i care about you"
and "you mean a lot to me"
smooches babe . . . . to hell with that

bullshit all nonsense when your know love is deceased
in a ration of portion of what is left of it, in my heart
do not beg for my "love back"
you misused it while at your disposal

puppy love is something else out of correlation
excitation is deep mediation between love and hate
reverberation is re-echoed sound of my sweet love passed on . . . .
to that next special goddess

Three Words

She passed modelling by the country side
Her tread I could feel vividly
Leaves rattled beneath her feet with admiration
Her smile caught my eye
Her glittering eyes glowed like diamond
The totality of her well defined beauty protrudes
Above my fantasies
Am I fit to woe?
Am I fit to be the suitor?
Does my three words suit her ears
Like a dream it all happened out of the blue
Her lips collides with mine for the first time
The gorgeously built figure now so close
How tantalizing is her touch
How sentimental is her laughter
How tranquillizing, her kiss among my lips

Am I fit to woe?
Am I fit to be the suitor?
Does my three words suit her ears

Dynamics of Love

the common pitfall of mating, dating and relating
its all ruins of dynamics of
a thing called love
such is not the chemistry
rather misconception of what has and still is love

Let man be man neither should woman act likes gals

the degree in psychology to figure woman out
is so overwhelming than the truth about the trinity
realise our judgement not to deceive our reasoning
about what woman want!!!
with a clear consciousness lets listen and learn
to embrace thou be loveth us so . . . .

Be not detrimental you same kind of man
woman are filled with envy, seeking to find
a different man to come salute
the attention they yawn for
affection is their craving . . .
man you better recognize this dynamics of love
The multitudes desire with admiration sighting

your eclipse of love . . . . she is the sunshine that makes you the
moon
resurrect the definition of love
coz gimmicks of life shall tell
without any sort of self hypnosis style "mind-fu"

Sternly K`Simon

Its compelling how woman are conditioned
as the initial awkwardness
was the 1st impression such that . . . deja-vu is not a dream
hence lust is not love break out of that state of limbo

The over ruling conviction of
What is to be or not to be
lie not or kiss them good bye
and your sorry ass shall pay the price
are you not worth her priceless love
you "um the man," "i got game"
who you trying to be "Casanova"

Been there, seen it and done it all

that and that
such demands portraying your distinct self
not that pretender, wanna be Don Juan
you stand to forfeit her that's your loss
Revealed here are the concealed dynamics of love

The inevitable Challenge

the inevitable challenge to contend for your love;
persevering
your objection i overruled
rejection i defied
only to be bivalent, and
append your demand for love, with your
charms i cant pretend to ignore

with your,
charms i cant pretend to ignore

the inevitable challenge to contend for your love;
pacifying
my obsession for you
i use my wits
only to challenge this predicament, of your
narcissism

of your,
narcissism

the inevitable challenge to contend for your love;
pleased to,
make your acquaintance
by the milk way
i wore a delightful smile
the compliment of your beauty, owes me
a mere Thank you

owes me,
a mere Thank you

the inevitable conclusion
of my challenge,
is to make you my black woman . . .
my black woman . . .

Blackwoman

black woman you caress the air waves with your sweet essence
hence your beauty shakes my stance with romance you bring
less not speak of the black woman's decency and forsake
ignorance
take heed for they shall not be resistance in their existence
you got heads turning even the presence of your shadow many
can sense
black woman you are the best Mona Lisa

you capture hearts like a lovers nest
the quest shall not be brought to rest
screen thee from the worst in your priority list

black woman you are the empress upon the throne of Africa

black woman you paint Africa with your brown skin
you hold no grudge for your heart is clean
behold as her true beauty pervades Africa like the word of God
shine on and claim your fame of respect, you gain, you earned
nations shall bow and salute
when your beauty slain their jealous slavery_idealogy they'll feel
the pain

black woman you are the one i adore

you are not a sham

black woman

Full moon

i meet u in e maze of ma life
i stepd on u lyk bubble gum of ma path
en thought, dat made me Adam n u Eve in the garden of eden
God must hav been crazy mad to laugh thunder
wen i c u at the end of a black n white rainbow lyk a fool
u r an ice breaker wen u create an avalanche 4 me
en u cum back lyk a shooting star across the full moon
the pacifier of ma soul
u drawn ma hart in shallow depth of ur luv n kindness
the murderer u hav become 2mi
u diffuse away as particle of matter dat i embrace 4 2min
en i hear heavens whisper; "she is just a dream"
doubtless 2 believe ma hart skipped a beat 4u at sum point
On a full moon

The break down

I am passed out like urination
And all my bones are out of joints, my heart is like wax
It is melted in the midst of my bowels
My strength is dried up like the well
And then hast brought me into the dust
Rust is breaking me down, I may tell my bones
They look and stare upon me
We are worked out and worn away like dead tires
Deliver my restless body from pain lord
My darling from the power of the devil
Show me thy medication and tools
To fix my breaking down soul
Fuel it up with love
I am breaking down
I need a pickup truck

Memories to a Smile

You ask if I smile,
when I think think think of you
But truth is
I don't think of you, not much at all
But memories are treasures in my chest
Stored

Stories of childhood in faraway places
(not physically, but in the way souls are carved
-or are souls moulded?
Is something added or taken away?
The appreciation of a drifting car with subtle
love overtones Calm
Appreciation gained that
I would never have realized on my own
Food shared from a plate.
We all eat, yet even in
this people try to keep themselves
separate

Or maybe it's just my culture.
Sandals chewen from a dog. Unusual sticky.
Unexpected Uberous Understanding
(and yes it's a word, I looked it up)
Poetry. Real. That speaks for itself.
Playing with a wide-eyed child, that once or twice
oozed into liquid sex
morphed into high school jerk
turned into trusted friend.

Sternly K`Simon

Alternating electricity
AV and what's the other one?
Or does it (he) really change?
It's just electrons.

Maybe it's just the way we (I) see it.
And so confusion
Which I don't mind
(or that's what the Buddhists tell us anyway)
But now what do I say?
Guarded stranger
or open friend
don't really mind rejection
(if an open heart can even be rejected.
It's just the closed ones
Walls used to prod poke bleed inward
But no walls—no weapons!

-———enlightenment)
Just confusion. Want all to be happy
but what is appropriate here?
So smile?—no.
Just a memory,
strung like pearls,
(imperfect though, not perfect ones)
And a moment's inspiration to write.

Phenomena

The idea of mine

i stand wide asunder to where the rivers meet
leaning on the walls of you against the world
the idea of mine,
you mocked excuse you . . .
your torments in reverse . . .

all come back to me now, like memories
resting on the comfort of this life is about you
what about me?
the idea of mine
you mocked excuse you . . .
your torments in reverse . . .

such is life, the shadows of us leave it too
complaining how you want heaven on earth
got me guessing, the idea of mine
you mocked excuse you . . .
your torments in reverse . . . x2

my idea was to celibate
on the debate you want to fornicate
devious to the idea of mine
you mocked excuse you . . .
your torments in reverse . . . x2

Incomplete

The retarded simile of my weirdness
A place where death does not reside, the metaphor
My poor soul has distressed and can't find rest
This uplifted spirit is in a quest
Contemplating suicide i cut my wrist
Incomplete rhymes seem my best
Cast are times then,
Now! The beast in me has power null to be tamed
It has my mind set
Nailed to the cross
Then it all comes back
To feast in my memories
Restraining mine heart with orders
Isolating me to a pensive mood

In a trance my soul being was left unconscious
And because its a pity
No heaven for a lost soul
Incomplete
My shutters never close sleeping or awake
Afraid because i can't find peace within
Could i perhaps meditate deeply?
Visualize and realize
Where do i go from here

Sternly K` Simon

emotionally incapacitated

essence of mine, painted with slander
When i feel a dark cloud over me
Walks of my life are dead ends
Pieces to my puzzle are missing the star of Pisces
And i hate the fact that
Um incomplete like a bald's

"Come"

i told i'll come
riding on a black stallion without a saddle
anchored by your real . . . appeal concealed
on a chariot from ancient times
i shall surpass myself to enchant you
when i come or rather should i seem macho
"sansei" to what made me come here
karma sutra of my de javu
it happened!
I came on July 19th from a ship without a captain
from sea shore, i saw you from afar
looking incredibly immaculate
crafted only from the finest South African pine
for this thought was long embedded in mind
now the day has made it real
intriguing massive vibes never felt before
to the clouds to even turn and stare aroused
the morning sun burning candles for romance
we share,
as i come tapping and clapping hands
with my tip-toe shoes and
the ground grew a pure silk mood
to welcome sigh out of your way of pleasure
my affectionate attention

now i come . . .
dressed on my nice khaki skin suite
emanating pleasant smells of a true black man
fusion, with the air you'll breath when I'm close to come
a potion of my presence
will quench your thirst of missing me when um gone
I'll come again here were i belong
when i come trees falling leaves
skies hallowing clear remaining cloudless
time patiently waiting with you for me to come
i am coming, i am coming, just know that
like oceans spitting gallons of water its a flood on the land
and you will be soaking wet in the rain um coming with
Satisfied will be your hazel eyes,

pleased to see me come . . .

My redemption

it's about the time crime rates have to be brought to shame
seize far thou art brothers at war against one blood
for thy core of our rooted harmony shall be peace
grant nonetheless the youth weapons of mass destruction
teach the children right
do not forsake their conscious mind nourishment of development
nurture Africa mothers of this earth
otherwise it shall be our perishment

I've spoken when not single a soul could
with the sound of this black child's echo
the wicked shall flee of course

I've spoken when words where not easy to find
bring back what is rightfully mine

I've seen the vision
I've the light
say no to war and more to life
burn the guns ammunition and throwaway the knifes
and burn corruption out of my sight

its about the time of truth the life blood of trust
if we don't trust in HIM who else
black people lets seek our way before we end up elsewhere
Babylon is our curse and we are lucky to be blessed
if we don't stand for anything we stand for nothing
I've seen them depopulate Africa
they come with the negative missionaries to hurt our positive
culture
nothing they do is ever look-active

my trouble of today
I choose my redemption
my blessings flow like the river Nile
my tragedy and my dismay

I've spoken when my sunshine was stolen by the dark
this dark complexion is our true reflection
I've spoken when winter comes spring time
but man never change as true colours they will reflect their
identity

lord!!!
how long shall they vanish black people
while we stand aside and look
some say is just a part of it
non but our self can free our minds
redemption poems is all i utter

Thou art: who I am

thou art, in the book shelf
multitudes judge thee by the cover
shall the verdict be; True/False about me

behold when i standout like a relief sculpture piece
this character is well brewed as the finest wine
personality portrayed is a true reflection of my kind
laying below the roots of this Black Child
I speak words of great eloquence in a few breath's

thou art, in wonderland
lord knows thee stands by the still waters
shall him look elsewhere; who have i become

thy complexion is not my completion
for I ought to chant a redemption song
filling my spiritual cup with his blessing to the brim
who shall i fear when he is standing by
i tremble not, working tall i stumble barely, nor shall i crumble

thou art, my testimony
shall be: to be or not to be
my words will be found on ancient scrolls

i despise pretenders around me proclaiming my life
living in vanity is not sanity for the conscious ones
simplicity i use to survive but many find it difficult

Sternly K` Simon

thou art, be who i am
change shall not come about like weather
confident i am in everything that i do
oh yes! my Lord my Father

i come from a place where you never tell a thing
when you know it
even if you have it
you know not to show it

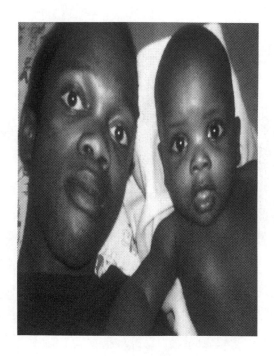

Until . . .
the End

What are friends for

.... Friends is a killer ....
What are friends for???
If they don't feel your distress the lord will be our fortress
.... drooling ....
My heart shedding one little tears for me
.... Liaising on tissues and below ....

Mourning about death and grief; the going was tough
what are friends for???
.... they should be liquidating ....
Many are gone the remaining to the shoulder
are few, um isolated when they seem collaborated without me
.... Their understanding of friendship gone-away with
ignorance ....
when lost; my 1 and only parent

such is life::::such life:::::::such is life:::::::::
When i say a word or two to them
they are framed surprised like wall pictures
Um not like Oliver Twist; if you catch this line
Some feel sorry as if i don't enjoy my company

Yesterday was my last teen days
Today is my birthday; but known celebrate it for its sake
. . . . What are friends for ??? . . . .
fortunately that made me stronger
That is why um still going like coal engine of 1969 training
Is the love of the common people
my grandmother comforting words
:::
What are friends for??? thats my question
. . . . we are better off without the enemies we keep close . . . .
. . . . and call them friends . . . .

Another tear i cry

as the day unfolds sunshine and darkness falls upon me
when his war is over freedom prevails across his soul
this place many dread and city lights they dream of
doors of heaven maybe open but not for all
rather this memories shall torment all as we try to move on
The moment of silence has come, lets pay respect
another tear i cry
dry cry even tells
even my heart cries but who cares
who cares no one but myself
Things do happen words can't explain
Is just one of them days, lost in the midst of death
RIP my brother
they is a heaven where in paradise you'll meet mama
another tear i cry
dry cry even tells
even my heart cries but who cares
who cares no one but myself
Things do happen words can't explain
Is just one of them days, lost in the midst of death

How much loss can this troubled heart of mine bear
Um just a mere child God don't take them all away
Even if your timing is the best one, for that i trust in thee
Spare my soul oh Jah for I am worried this time it will not heal
I never thought of death until you took my mama, now my
brother
another tear i cry
dry cry even tells
even my heart cries but who cares
who cares no one but myself
Things do happen words can't explain
Is just one of them days, lost in the midst of death

As they mourn, i will be celebrating your life big brother
Life goes on
such is life
I will console myself and keep my head up because you thought
me well
Um proud, you made me a real man

Endless

where to begin at this juncture
the rapture of my endless thinking,
"picture"
long endless strokes paint my life exposure
feeling blue;
sure this is a fracture to the brain
my brain;
departure,
worries flee to assure me peace of mind
rain drops in a marathon race,

Sternly K` Simon

in my head
chasing away this misty clouds upon mine eyez
mountains of my troubles crying waterfalls
tree branches swaying to the wind blows
breaking down chains of my endless data
status perpetrated this vision
"endless"
seasons married to divorce another
the fire burned whilst i watch flames dancing
during the rebuke of my down moment
the dispute was endless
to consume me some more . . . .
i began on a plain page
why should i complain . . . .
wearing a skeptical smile;
where they is endless hope, on what um living for . . . .
This endless thoughts
As though
The end of my life perspective
I cannot visualize . . . .

Nothing at All

did you get that message
which is not like an aphrodisiac
with letters of the alphabet that wrote your zodiac
that you don't believe in, its diverse metaphor still
did you get that message
which is not like a sentimental gesture
with lack of chronological message line
yet delivered to you and to me
that was not coincidence anticipated okay
did you get that message
which had rough like lines not rhymes
with built in rapport with you
on a sensible level to communicate killing the silence of the lamb
"quotes" and parables of the message with no simile
did you get that message
which read not from the holy bible nor the Al-Quran
with words not much like love or hate
perhaps it was meant to be like a subtle whispers
in the darkest of your thoughts the message said,
"nothing at all"

A Secrets
Told To 1 is Al

Loveless brother

I've seen heaven when you were in hell

I've done good against your evil doings

I've found my way when you where lost

I've earned my respect where you did not respect yourself

I've foreseen where we are heading and we leaving you behind

I've stole hearts of many girls while you broke them apart
I've condomized to avoid what infected you
I've found love even in the darkest of places
and i pity you loveless black brother
I've made them proud why did you have to disappoint them
I've got my life together
but you need to get your act together

I've charisma like Casanova that's why they feel me more, to fear you

I've seen you frown when i am smiling like a horse at your girl

I've danced to the sound of the beat and you had no rhythm at all

I've treated her like a lady since you were not man enough for her

I've to say this that you are a bad man

His Fables

For you are not around

for you are not around anymore
you were the ground underneath his bare feet
behind him we saw a strong man
the blazing heat in his nervous was you sunshine
Your warmth and beauty signified a warm welcome

for you are not around
the demise was or is now or never
he was not haste to waste time
but to endure you was his endeavor
his doubts + worries about you he shun to devour his love to you

foreseen outcomes of this disloyalty
was written
before it was tabled
biased with prejudice to man
woman were re vowed the power to rule emotions
when her physical phenotype sufficed man
drawn was her line of truth
the truth unsaid deeply concealed to be unrevealed
blind folded then man walked across this line
with no walking stick

for now you are not around
his crises is now
loneliness is his dungeon of ever finding someone like you
feel his emptiness like an empty drum making noise
oh! how he misses you gravity, the moon is not like you earth
angel

for you are not around
for you are not around

His Story

decades of his untold story
added up centuries of mercy
still the man prowls
the orbitals of thousands
felt feelings
over she;

un-responding doubted cupid heart
over desire;
fluctuation of lust long lasted
perhaps deeds are due
prepaid tribute to the
heart that skipped huddles of beats
in the cradle
what's shall she be called
Sarah Conor at their meeting corner
he waited;

breathing the midnight strewn
of-cause she caused him perplexed
of like devil awakened from un-spread-ed sheets
bestowed her resentfulness to the fact
a man macho never halts persuading more
civil and governed by his want not need
of her;

seems hard headed to re-act to rejection
acting upon a story fancying her;
his fiction
nah we all love whom don't return our love
no surprise he could not reckon
let bygones be bygones
she! in her depicted you not for her
botheration in him bothered anchor
the extent he went over overwhelming
proposing a girl ever over and over again
he done soaked drowning in his small brain
to her palatable body to skin
nothing like it;
seeking lingered to perspective
in getting her to say Yes! vain
fallen wilderness of another tatterdemalion heart
on purpose because she told him NO NO NO
she exerts enormous power, doesn't she
regardless he got bitter to the extent to call
her names
that cannot be exquisitely
be pronounced by this poem
his story 2 words put together minus 1 's' history
his own impeded diluted sorry ass
we told him a heart is brickle
the divine truth, he will be single
that we all presume
didn't she say boy
we can just be friends
indeed how polite and nice could she be
insult to him another skirt of the hundreds
dares to make him her door mat

it was said he went bizarre crazy
when little Missy was drawing away
swifting to the sunset
where her heart will regain a break
mr man! pondering attack strategy on2 her
his flow-like no-retreat no-surrender
the cup cake was the enemy
she brought no weapon to his fight
lasted 4years forfeited soldier defeated
but still alive . . . was he
forget his tactics and money spent on this girls
its embarrassing
to even tell that part of the his story
because the past is the wilderness of horrors
desire of a man is an extremist ultra stimulating
to the poet"
articulated by the boy utterly saying three words
i love you
girl said boy
you scarring the sweetness from the diaphragm of me
we could never be love in the romance making
boy said, how so!
Shorty babey boo
you trigger pull words from my mouth stammering
always your lips are glimmering
to melt Antarctic that's why i want you
she said i don't want you near my Venus alien from mars
in his craving of yesteryear's for her "
reminiscing yesterdays heard of rejection
twilight 2the new saga
hunger of yawning like desire not deserving the girl
killing the drawn feeling glinting with impishness
love note

Sternly K` Simon

uncomplimentary to the contrary
affirming but blasphemous
when his story
was published an impeachment notice was written
and he took an obsession oath
possessed by an assumption spell from her
she could love him one untold day